# Vegan Gluten-Free Baking Totally Guilt-Free!

*Healthy and Delicious, 100% Vegan and Gluten-Free Dessert Recipes You Will Love*

By Kira Novac (ISBN: 978-1-80095-033-7)

Copyright ©Kira Novac 2015

www.amazon.com/author/kira-novac

All rights reserved. No part of this publication may be reproduced, stored in a retrieval system, or transmitted, in any form or by any means, electronic, mechanical, photocopying, recording or otherwise, without the prior written permission of the author and the publishers.

The scanning, uploading, and distribution of this book via the Internet, or via any other means, without the permission of the author is illegal and punishable by law. Please purchase only authorized electronic editions, and do not participate in or encourage electronic piracy of copyrighted materials.

All information in this book has been carefully researched and checked for factual accuracy. However, the author and publishers make no warranty, expressed or implied, that the information contained herein is appropriate for every individual, situation or purpose, and assume no responsibility for errors or omission. The reader assumes the risk and full responsibility for all actions, and the author will not be held liable for any loss or damage, whether consequential, incidental, and special or otherwise, that may result from the information presented in this publication.

A physician has not written the information in this book. Before making any serious dietary changes, I advise you to consult with your physician first.

# Table of contents

Introduction ........................................................................... 1
   About the Recipes ............................................................ 4
PART 1:  Muffins and Breakfast Bread Recipes ........................... 8
   Almond Flour Blueberry Muffins ...................................... 9
   Chocolate Raspberry Muffins ......................................... 12
   Coconut Flour Apple Cinnamon Muffins ....................... 15
   Fluffy Coconut Oil Biscuits ............................................. 18
   Blueberry Coconut Scones ............................................. 20
   Spiced Pumpkin Oat Muffins .......................................... 23
   Cinnamon Banana and Walnut Muffins ......................... 26
   Vegan Herb Biscuits ....................................................... 29
   Vegan Carrot Cake Muffins ............................................ 31
   Cinnamon Apple Scones ................................................ 34
   Double Chocolate Chip Muffins .................................... 37
PART 2:  Vegan Gluten-Free Cookies and Bars .......................... 40
   Oatmeal Raisin Cookies ................................................. 41
   Fudgy Coconut Flour Brownies ..................................... 44
   Easy Banana Oat Cookies .............................................. 47
   Vegan Chocolate Chip Cookies ..................................... 49
   Chocolate Chip Blondies ............................................... 52
   Gluten-Free Peanut Butter Cookies ............................... 55
   Vegan Double Chocolate Cookies ................................. 57
   Peanut Butter Chocolate Brownies ................................ 60
   Gluten-Free Almond Cookies ........................................ 63
   Maple Oatmeal Walnut Cookies .................................... 65
PART 3:  Vegan Gluten-Free Cakes, Cupcakes and Quick Breads 68

Vegan Chocolate Cupcakes ............................................................. 69
Gluten-Free Chocolate Zucchini Bread ...................................... 72
Gluten-Free Sponge Cake ............................................................. 75
Vanilla Bean Cupcakes .................................................................. 77
Easy Cinnamon Pumpkin Bread ................................................. 80
Chocolate Coconut Cupcakes ..................................................... 83
Vanilla Strawberry Sheet Cake .................................................. 86
Gluten-Free Carob Chip Banana Bread ................................... 89
Raspberry Coconut Cupcakes .................................................... 92
Lemon Blueberry Cake .................................................................. 95
Vegan Cinnamon Zucchini Bread .............................................. 98
Conclusion ....................................................................................... 102
To post an honest review ........................................................... 105
Recommended Reading .............................................................. 106

# Introduction

When you switch to the vegan diet, you may be worried about whether or not you will still be able to eat your favorite foods. While you might have to make some big changes to your diet, there are plenty of vegan alternatives out there for traditional foods. You can still enjoy things like pancakes, muffins, even omelets for breakfast as well as hearty soups, stews, and entrees – even decadent desserts! The vegan diet is an excellent choice if you are looking for a way to improve your health and vitality and, with the recipes included in this book, you won't feel like you are making a sacrifice.

Another diet that has recently skyrocketed in popularity is the gluten-free diet. While many people are forced to switch to this diet out of medical necessity resulting from gluten allergies or intolerance, some people are making the switch simply because they think it is a healthy alternative to the modern Western diet. The truth of the matter is that the gluten-free diet is not a magical solution for weight loss or health problems, but you can use it as a tool to achieve your health and wellness goals. The gluten-free diet can even be combined with the vegan diet, if you like!

The vegan gluten-free diet might take a little bit of getting used to because you can no longer eat animal products like meat, eggs, and dairy – you also need to avoid gluten-containing grains like wheat, barley and rye. If you take the time to really learn about this diet, however, you will find that there are still plenty of vegan gluten-free options out there. You can still enjoy tasty muffins and pancakes made with gluten-free flours as well as vegan versions of your favorite soups and stews. The vegan gluten-free diet can be adapted to include everything from pasta and rice dishes to indulgent desserts.

Once you make the switch to the vegan gluten-free diet you shouldn't be surprised if you feel your body start to change. Removing processed grains and animal products from your diet can work wonders for your digestion and your body as a whole. You may find that you have more energy during the day and that you no longer suffer from food cravings. The vegan gluten-free diet can be used as a tool for weight loss because many of the foods included in the diet are naturally low in calories but high in nutrition. Just be sure to mind your portions and make an effort to follow a balanced diet.

If you are ready to give the vegan gluten-free diet a try, this book is the perfect place to start. In the pages of this book you will find a collection of dozens of vegan gluten-free recipes from pancakes to pasta and everything in between.

So what are you waiting for? Pick a recipe and start cooking!

## *About the Recipes*

The cup measurement I use is the American cup measurement.

If you don't have American Cup measures, just use a metric or imperial liquid measuring jug and fill your jug with your ingredient to the corresponding level. Here's how to go about it:

1 American Cup = 250ml = 8 fl.oz

**For example:**

If a recipe calls for 1 cup of almonds, simply place your almonds into your measuring jug until it reaches the 250 ml/8oz mark.

I know that different countries use different measurements and I wanted to make things simple for you. I have also noticed that very often those who are used to American cup measurements complain about metric measurements and vice versa. However, if you apply what I have just explained, you will find it easy to use both.

Also, remember that you can always e-mail me and ask for help. I will also be happy to get your feedback:

kira.novac@kiraglutenfreerecipes.com

# Free Complimentary Recipe eBook

Thank you so much for taking an interest in my work!

As a thank you, I would love to offer you a free complimentary recipe eBook to help you achieve vibrant health. It will teach you how to prepare amazingly tasty and healthy gluten-free treats so that you never feel deprived or bored again!

As a special bonus, you will be able to receive all my future books (kindle format) for free or only $0.99.

**Download your free recipe eBook here:**

http://bit.ly/gluten-free-desserts-book

# PART 1:

# Muffins and Breakfast Bread Recipes

# Almond Flour Blueberry Muffins

**Servings**: 12

**Ingredients**:

- 2 tablespoons of ground flaxseed
- 5 tablespoons of warm water
- ½ cup of unsweetened almond milk
- 1 teaspoon of apple cider vinegar
- 1 ¾ teaspoons of baking soda

- ½ cup of old-fashioned oats
- ½ cup of blanched almond flour
- ½ teaspoon of salt
- ¾ cups of gluten-free flour blend
- ¾ cups of unsweetened applesauce
- 4 tablespoons of melted coconut oil
- 4 to 6 tablespoons of pure maple syrup
- ¼ cup of organic cane sugar
- 1 ½ cups of fresh blueberries

**Instructions**:

1. Preheat your oven to a temperature of 375°F and line a 12-cup muffin pan using paper liners – you can also just spray it with cooking spray.
2. Whisk together your flaxseed and warm water in a small bowl – let it rest for 5 minutes.
3. Combine your almond milk and vinegar in another bowl and stir well.
4. Let the mixture sit for 2 to 3 minutes then stir in the baking soda and set it aside.
5. Combine your applesauce, coconut oil, maple syrup, and sugar in a mixing bowl.

6. Whisk in your flaxseed mixture then stir in your almond milk mixture.
7. In another bowl, stir together your oats and almond flour along with the salt and then whisk them into the wet ingredients.
8. Toss your blueberries with the gluten-free flour blend and then stir your blueberries into the batter until the mixture it just combined.
9. Spoon the batter into your prepared muffin pan, filling each cup about ¾ of the way full.
10. Bake the muffins for between 18 and 24 minutes until a toothpick that you insert in the center comes out clean.
11. Cool the muffins for about 5 minutes in the pan and then transfer them to a cooling rack to cool all the way.

## *Chocolate Raspberry Muffins*

**Servings**: 12

**Ingredients**:

- 2 tablespoons of ground flaxseed
- 5 tablespoons of warm water
- ¼ cup of all-natural almond butter
- 2 tablespoons of melted coconut oil
- ½ cup organic cane sugar

- 2 teaspoons of vanilla extract
- 1 cup of unsweetened almond milk
- ½ cup of sifted coconut flour
- 5 tablespoons of cocoa powder (unsweetened)
- 2 ¼ teaspoons of baking powder
- Pinch of salt
- 1 cup of fresh raspberries

**Instructions**:

1. Preheat your oven to a temperature of 350°F and line a 12-cup muffin pan using paper liners – you can also just spray it with cooking spray.
2. Whisk together your flaxseed and water in a small bowl then set aside for 5 minutes.
3. Combine your almond butter and coconut oil with the sugar and vanilla extract in a mixing bowl.
4. Beat those ingredients until they are well combined.
5. Whisk in your flaxseed mixture and then stir in the almond milk while you are beating the mixture on low speed.
6. In a separate bowl, stir together your coconut flour and cocoa powder with the baking powder and salt.
7. Add the dry ingredient mixture in small batches while you beat the wet ingredient mixture.

8. Beat until the mixture is well combined and then fold in your fresh raspberries.
9. Spoon the finished batter into your prepared pan, filling each cup about ¾ of the way full.
10. Bake your muffins for between 18 and 20 minutes until a knife that you insert in the middle comes out clean.
11. Cool your muffins for 5 minutes in the pan and then remove them to a cooling rack to finish cooling.

# Coconut Flour Apple Cinnamon Muffins

**Servings**: 12

**Ingredients**:

- 2 tablespoons of ground flaxseed
- 5 tablespoons of warm water
- ½ cup plus 1 tablespoon of coconut flour
- 2 teaspoons of baking powder
- 1 teaspoon of ground cinnamon

- ¼ cup of all-natural almond butter
- ½ cup of organic cane sugar
- 2 tablespoons of melted coconut oil
- 3 teaspoons of vanilla extract
- 1 cup of unsweetened almond milk
- ½ cup of chopped up apple

**Instructions**:

1. Preheat your oven to a temperature of 350°F and line a 12-cup muffin pan using paper liners – you can also just spray it with cooking spray.
2. Combine your flaxseed and water in a small bowl and let it rest for 5 minutes.
3. In another mixing bowl, stir together your coconut flour with the baking powder and cinnamon.
4. Combine your almond butter and sugar with your coconut oil and vanilla in another bowl.
5. Stir your mixture until it is smooth and then stir in the flaxseed mixture from the bowl.
6. While stirring the mixture, slowly pour in your almond milk and then stir in your dry ingredient mixture.
7. Fold in your chopped apples and then spoon the batter into your prepared pan, filling each cup about ¾ full.

8. Bake your muffins for between 18 and 22 minutes until a knife comes out clean when you insert it in the middle.
9. Cool your muffins for 5 minutes in your pan and then put them on a cooling rack to finish cooling.

## *Fluffy Coconut Oil Biscuits*

**Servings**: 12

**Ingredients**:

- 4 cups of all-purpose gluten-free flour blend
- ¼ to 1/3 cup organic sugar
- 1 ½ tablespoons of baking powder
- 1 teaspoon of salt
- 1 ½ cups of unsweetened almond milk

- 1 cup of coconut oil (room temperature)

**Instructions**:

1. Preheat your oven to a temperature of 400°F.
2. Combine the gluten-free flour with the sugar, baking powder and salt in a mixing bowl.
3. Stir the ingredients well and then whisk in your almond milk.
4. Make sure the mixture is well combined then stir in the coconut oil until you are left with a crumbly mixture.
5. Take handfuls of the mixture and shape them into a round biscuit, compressing the dough without over-kneading it.
6. Place the biscuits on a parchment-lined baking sheet and bake them for 16 to 20 minutes.
7. The biscuits should be lightly golden in color on top.
8. Cool the biscuits on a cooling rack before serving them.

## *Blueberry Coconut Scones*

**Servings**: 8

**Ingredients**:

- 1 ½ cups of brown rice flour
- ½ cup of tapioca starch
- ¼ cup of organic cane sugar
- ½ tablespoon of baking powder
- ½ teaspoon of salt

- 1/3 cup of vegetable shortening
- 1 cup of fresh blueberries
- ¼ cup of unsweetened shredded coconut
- 2 tablespoons of chia seeds
- 2 tablespoons of hot water
- ½ cup of unsweetened almond milk

**Instructions**:

1. Preheat your oven to a temperature of 425°F and put a piece of parchment paper over a cookie sheet.
2. Combine your rice flour and tapioca starch in a mixing bowl with your sugar, baking powder and salt.
3. Add the shortening and stir it in with a fork until you get a crumbly mixture.
4. Stir in your blueberries and coconut then set the mixture aside.
5. Whisk together your chia seeds and water in a small bowl then pour it into a blender.
6. Blend in the almond milk and then stir the blended mixture into your blueberry mixture.
7. Shape the resulting dough into a ball using your hands and then flatted it into a round disc.

8. Cut your dough into 8 slices and then place them on your cookie sheet, keeping the slices separated.
9. Bake your scones for between 22 and 26 minutes until they are golden brown.

# Spiced Pumpkin Oat Muffins

**Servings**: 12

**Ingredients**:

- 2 cups of gluten-free all-purpose flour blend
- 1 ½ cups of organic cane sugar
- 1 teaspoon of baking soda
- 1 teaspoon of ground cinnamon
- ½ teaspoon of ground nutmeg

- ½ teaspoon of salt
- ¾ cups of canned coconut milk
- 1 teaspoon of organic cider vinegar
- ¼ cup of olive oil
- 2 tablespoons of agave nectar
- 1 cup of pumpkin puree
- 1 ½ teaspoons of vanilla extract
- ½ cup of gluten-free oats

**Instructions**:

1. Preheat your oven to a temperature of 350°F and line a 12-cup muffin pan using paper liners – you can also just spray it with cooking spray.
2. Combine your gluten-free flour and sugar in a large mixing bowl with your baking soda, cinnamon, nutmeg, and salt.
3. In another bowl stir together your coconut milk and your apple cider vinegar.
4. Let the mixture sit for about 2 minutes then stir in your olive oil, agave, pumpkin, and vanilla extract.
5. Stir your dry ingredients into the wet ingredient mixture until it is combined well.

6. Spoon your muffin batter into the muffin cups, filling each one about ¾ of the way full and then sprinkle the oats on top.
7. Bake your pumpkin muffins for between 25 and 32 minutes until a toothpick that you insert in the center comes out clean.
8. Cool the muffins for about 5 minutes in the pan and then transfer them to a cooling rack to cool all the way.

## Cinnamon Banana and Walnut Muffins

**Servings**: 12

**Ingredients**:

- 2 tablespoons of ground flaxseed
- 5 tablespoons of warm water
- ½ cup of unsweetened almond milk
- 1 teaspoon of apple cider vinegar
- 1 ¾ teaspoons of baking soda

- ½ cup of old-fashioned oats
- ½ cup of blanched almond flour
- 1 ½ teaspoons of ground cinnamon
- ½ teaspoon of salt
- ¾ cups of gluten-free flour blend
- ¾ cups of mashed up bananas
- 4 tablespoons of melted coconut oil
- 4 to 6 tablespoons of agave nectar
- ¼ cup of organic cane sugar
- 1 cup of chopped up walnuts

**Instructions**:

1. Preheat your oven to a temperature of 375°F and line a 12-cup muffin pan using paper liners – you can also just spray it with cooking spray.
2. Whisk together your flaxseed and warm water in a small bowl – let it rest for 5 minutes.
3. Combine your almond milk and vinegar in another bowl and stir well.
4. Let the mixture sit for 2 to 3 minutes then stir in the baking soda and set it aside.
5. Combine your mashed apples, coconut oil, agave nectar, and sugar in a mixing bowl.

6. Whisk in your flaxseed mixture then stir in your almond milk mixture.
7. In another bowl, stir together your oats and almond flour along with the cinnamon and salt and then whisk them into the wet ingredients.
8. Toss your walnuts with the gluten-free flour blend and then stir your walnuts into the batter until the mixture it just combined.
9. Spoon the batter into your prepared muffin pan, filling each cup about ¾ of the way full.
10. Bake the muffins for between 18 and 24 minutes until a toothpick that you insert in the center comes out clean.
11. Cool the muffins for about 5 minutes in the pan and then transfer them to a cooling rack to cool all the way.

## *Vegan Herb Biscuits*

**Servings**: 12

**Ingredients**:

- 4 cups of all-purpose gluten-free flour blend
- ¼ to 1/3 cup organic sugar
- 1 ½ tablespoons of baking powder
- 1 teaspoon of salt
- 2 teaspoons of dried rosemary

- 2 teaspoons of dried thyme
- 1 ½ cups of unsweetened almond milk
- 1 cup of coconut oil (room temperature)

**Instructions**:

1. Preheat your oven to a temperature of 400°F.
2. Combine the gluten-free flour with the sugar, baking powder and salt in a mixing bowl along with the dried herbs.
3. Stir the ingredients well and then whisk in your almond milk.
4. Make sure the mixture is well combined then stir in the coconut oil until you are left with a crumbly mixture.
5. Take handfuls of the mixture and shape them into a round biscuit, compressing the dough without over-kneading it.
6. Place the biscuits on a parchment-lined baking sheet and bake them for 16 to 20 minutes.
7. The biscuits should be lightly golden in color on top.
8. Cool the biscuits on a cooling rack before serving them.

# Vegan Carrot Cake Muffins

**Servings**: 12

**Ingredients**:

- 1 ½ tablespoons of ground flaxseed
- 3 ½ tablespoons of warm water
- 1 large mashed-up banana
- 4 tablespoons of maple syrup
- 4 tablespoons of olive oil

- ½ cup of unsweetened applesauce
- ½ cup of organic cane sugar
- 1 ¼ cup of all-purpose gluten-free flour blend
- ½ cup of rolled oats
- ½ cup of almond flour
- 1 ½ teaspoons of baking soda
- 1 teaspoon of ground cinnamon
- ½ teaspoon of salt
- ½ cup of unsweetened almond milk
- 1 cup of grated carrots

**Instructions**:

1. Preheat your oven to a temperature of 375°F and line a 12-cup muffin pan using paper liners – you can also just spray it with cooking spray.
2. Whisk together your ground flaxseed with water in a small bowl and let it sit for 5 minutes.
3. Place your mashed-up banana in a mixing bowl and stir it together with your maple syrup and olive oil.
4. Stir in your flaxseed mixture as well as the applesauce and the sugar.
5. In another bowl, combine your gluten-free flour and oats with the almond flour, baking soda, cinnamon and the salt.

6. Stir your dry ingredients into the wet ingredients and then whisk in your almond milk.
7. Fold in your grated carrots until the mixture is just combined.
8. Spoon your muffin batter into your prepared pan, filling each cup about ¾ of the way full.
9. Bake your muffins for between 30 and 35 minutes until a knife that you put in the middle comes out clean.
10. Cool your muffins for about 10 to 15 minutes in the pan and then take them out to cool the rest of the way.
11. Optional: sprinkle some cane sugar on top.

# Cinnamon Apple Scones

**Servings**: 8

**Ingredients**:

- 1 ½ cups of brown rice flour
- ½ cup of tapioca starch
- ¼ cup of organic cane sugar
- 1 teaspoon of ground cinnamon
- ½ tablespoon of baking powder

- ½ teaspoon of salt
- 1/3 cup of vegetable shortening
- 1 cup of chopped apples
- 2 tablespoons of chia seeds
- 2 tablespoons of hot water
- ½ cup of unsweetened almond milk

**Instructions**:

1. Preheat your oven to a temperature of 425°F and put a piece of parchment paper over a cookie sheet.
2. Combine your rice flour and tapioca starch in a mixing bowl with your sugar, cinnamon, baking powder and salt.
3. Add the shortening and stir it in with a fork until you get a crumbly mixture.
4. Stir in your chopped apples and then set the mixture aside.
5. Whisk together your chia seeds and water in a small bowl then pour it into a blender.
6. Blend in the almond milk and then stir the blended mixture into your blueberry mixture.
7. Shape the resulting dough into a ball using your hands and then flatted it into a round disc.
8. Cut your dough into 8 slices and then place them on your cookie sheet, keeping the slices separated.

9. Bake your scones for between 22 and 26 minutes until they are golden brown.

## *Double Chocolate Chip Muffins*

**Servings**: 12

**Ingredients**:

- 2 tablespoons of ground flaxseed
- 5 tablespoons of warm water
- ¼ cup of all-natural almond butter
- 2 tablespoons of melted coconut oil
- ½ cup organic cane sugar

- 3 teaspoons of vanilla extract
- 1 cup of unsweetened almond milk
- ½ cup of sifted coconut flour
- 6 tablespoons of cocoa powder (unsweetened)
- 2 ¼ teaspoons of baking powder
- Pinch of salt
- 1/3 to ½ cup carob chips (dairy-free chocolate chips)

**Instructions**:

1. Preheat your oven to a temperature of 350°F and line a 12-cup muffin pan using paper liners – you can also just spray it with cooking spray.
2. Whisk together your flaxseed and water in a small bowl then set aside for 5 minutes.
3. Combine your almond butter and coconut oil with the sugar and vanilla extract in a mixing bowl.
4. Beat those ingredients until they are well combined.
5. Whisk in your flaxseed mixture and then stir in the almond milk while you are beating the mixture on low speed.
6. In a separate bowl, stir together your coconut flour and cocoa powder with the baking powder and salt.
7. Add the dry ingredient mixture in small batches while you beat the wet ingredient mixture.

8. Beat until the mixture is well combined and then fold in your carob chips.
9. Spoon the finished batter into your prepared pan, filling each cup about ¾ of the way full.
10. Bake your muffins for between 18 and 20 minutes until a knife that you insert in the middle comes out clean.
11. Cool your muffins for 5 minutes in the pan and then remove them to a cooling rack to finish cooling.

# PART 2:

# Vegan Gluten-Free Cookies and Bars

## *Oatmeal Raisin Cookies*

**Servings**: 16 to 18

**Ingredients**:

- 1 tablespoon of ground flaxseed
- 3 tablespoons of warm water
- 2 cups of old-fashioned oats
- 1 cup of all-purpose gluten-free flour blend
- 1 ½ teaspoons of ground cinnamon

- ¾ teaspoon of baking soda
- Pinch of salt
- ½ cup of vegan butter at room temperature
- ½ cup of organic cane sugar
- 1 teaspoon of vanilla extract
- 1 cup of seedless raisins

**Instructions:**

1. Preheat your oven to a temperature of 350°F and place a piece of parchment paper on a baking sheet.
2. Stir together your flaxseed and your water in a small bowl and let it sit for 5 minutes.
3. In another bowl, stir your oats together with your gluten-free flour and your cinnamon, baking soda, and salt.
4. In a separate bowl, use a stand mixer or hand mixer to beat the vegan butter with the sugar until it is fluffy.
5. Beat in your flaxseed mixture and the vanilla extract as well.
6. Slowly add your flour mixture while you are beating the batter until it is just combined.
7. Stir in your raisins and then drop the cookie dough onto the cookie sheet.
8. Make each cookie about 2 tablespoons worth of dough.

9. Bake your cookies for between 15 and 20 minutes until the edges of them are golden brown.

## *Fudgy Coconut Flour Brownies*

**Servings**: 10 to 12

**Ingredients**:

- 1 cup of canned coconut milk (light)
- ¼ cup of ground flaxseed
- 1 cup of vegan chocolate chips
- ½ cup of agave nectar
- 2 tablespoons of organic cane sugar

- 3 tablespoons of coconut oil
- 1 tablespoon of vanilla extract
- 1 cup minus 2 tablespoons of coconut flour
- 3 tablespoons of tapioca starch
- ½ teaspoon of baking powder
- ¼ teaspoon of baking soda
- ¼ teaspoon of salt
- ¼ cup of chopped dark chocolate

**Instructions**:

1. Preheat your oven to a temperature of 375°F and place a piece of parchment paper on the bottom of a square baking pan – grease it with cooking spray.
2. Put your coconut milk in a saucepan and heat it until it steams.
3. Pour the milk into a bowl and stir in your flaxseed and vegan chocolate chips.
4. Let the chocolate chips melt and then stir in the agave, sugar and oil as well as the vanilla extract.
5. Let the mixture sit for 5 minutes while you stir together your coconut flour, tapioca starch, baking powder, baking soda, and salt.

6. Stir the dry ingredients into the chocolate mixture until it is combined well.
7. Fold in your dark chocolate and then pour the batter into your baking pan.
8. Bake the brownies for between 22 and 25 minutes and then let them cool completely before you slice them.

## *Easy Banana Oat Cookies*

**Servings**: about 2 dozen

**Ingredients**:

- 1 cup of pitted dates
- 1 medium banana, peeled and chopped
- 2 tablespoons of almond butter
- ¾ cup of blanched almond flour
- ¾ cup of old fashioned oats

- ½ teaspoon of ground cinnamon
- ¼ cup of chopped up walnuts

**Instructions:**

1. Preheat your oven to a temperature of 350°F and place a piece of parchment paper on a baking sheet.
2. Put the dates in a food processor and blend them up well.
3. Add your bananas and your almond butter and blend it until it is combined well.
4. Pour in your almond flour, oats and cinnamon then pulse the mixture until it forms a kind of loose dough.
5. Transfer your dough into a mixing bowl – you might need to add a little more almond flour to make it stick together.
6. Stir in your chopped up walnuts and then put the dough in the fridge for 10 minutes.
7. Drop the dough using a tablespoon onto the cookie sheet.
8. Bake your cookies for between 15 and 18 minutes until the edges are brown.

## *Vegan Chocolate Chip Cookies*

**Servings**: about 2 dozen

**Ingredients**:

- 1 cup of organic cane sugar
- ½ cup of coconut oil
- ¼ cup of unsweetened almond milk
- ¼ cup of all-natural almond butter
- 2 tablespoons of ground flaxseed

- 2 teaspoons of vanilla extract
- 3 cups of oat flour
- 1 ¼ cups of blanched almond flour
- ¼ cup of arrowroot powder
- 1 ½ teaspoons of baking powder
- 1 ½ teaspoons of baking soda
- 1 teaspoon of salt

**Instructions**:

1. Preheat your oven to a temperature of 350°F and place a piece of parchment paper on a baking sheet.
2. Combine your sugar together with your coconut oil in a mixing bowl and beat it with a hand beater.
3. Add in your almond milk, almond butter and flaxseed as well as your vanilla – beat it until it is combined well.
4. In another bowl, stir together the rest of the ingredients except for your chocolate chips.
5. Add your dry ingredient mixture to your wet ingredients until it is combined well.
6. Fold in your chocolate chips and then chill your dough for 15 minutes.
7. Drop the dough using a tablespoon onto the cookie sheet.

8. Bake your cookies for between 12 and 15 minutes until the edges are brown.

## *Chocolate Chip Blondies*

**Servings**: 16 to 18

**Ingredients**:

- 1 tablespoon of ground flaxseed
- 3 tablespoons of warm water

- ½ cup of coconut butter, melted
- ½ cup of organic cane sugar
- 2 teaspoons of vanilla extract
- 1 tablespoon of agave nectar
- ½ teaspoon of baking soda
- Pinch of salt
- 3 teaspoons of tapioca starch
- 1 cup of oat flour
- ¾ cups of blanched almond flour
- 1/3 cup of vegan chocolate chips (more if needed)

**Instructions**:

1. Preheat your oven to a temperature of 350°F and place a piece of parchment paper on the bottom of a square baking pan – grease it with cooking spray.
2. Combine your flaxseed and your water in a large bowl and let it sit for 5 minutes.
3. Add your coconut butter and sugar as well as your vanilla extract and agave – stir it until it is combined well.
4. Stir in your baking soda and salt as well as your tapioca starch then stir in your chocolate chips.
5. Add your oat flour and almond flour to the wet ingredients and stir it until it forms a thick dough.

6. Spread your batter in the prepared pan and sprinkle with extra chocolate chips, if desired.
7. Cook the blondies for between 15 and 20 minutes until the edges are golden brown.

## *Gluten-Free Peanut Butter Cookies*

**Servings**: about 2 dozen

**Ingredients**:

- 2 cups of all-natural peanut butter
- 2 cups of organic cane sugar
- 1 tablespoon of vanilla extract
- 1 1/3 cups of oat flour
- 2 teaspoons of baking soda

- ½ teaspoon of salt

**Instructions**:

1. Preheat your oven to a temperature of 350°F and place a piece of parchment paper on a baking sheet.
2. Combine your peanut butter and sugar in a mixing bowl and beat it with a hand mixer until it is fluffy.
3. Beat in your vanilla extract for about 30 seconds.
4. In another bowl, combine together your oat flour, baking soda and salt.
5. Add your dry ingredients a little at a time to the wet mixture, beating it with the hand mixer.
6. Roll your dough out by hand into small balls and place them on the baking sheet.
7. Flatten the cookies a little and then bake them for between 8 and 10 minutes until the edges are browned.

## *Vegan Double Chocolate Cookies*

**Servings**: about 2 dozen

**Ingredients**:

- 2 tablespoons of ground flaxseed
- 6 tablespoons of warm water
- ½ cup of almond butter
- ½ cup of coconut oil
- 1 1/3 cups of organic cane sugar

- 1 teaspoons of vanilla extract
- 1 teaspoon of baking soda
- 1 teaspoon of baking powder
- 1 teaspoon of salt
- 1/3 cup of cocoa powder (unsweetened)
- 3 cups of old-fashioned oats
- 1 tablespoon of almond milk
- 1 ½ cups of vegan chocolate chips

**Instructions**:

1. Preheat your oven to a temperature of 350°F and place a piece of parchment paper on a baking sheet.
2. Combine your flaxseed and your water in a medium bowl and let it sit for 5 minutes.
3. Add your almond butter, coconut oil and sugar along with the vanilla extract and beat it smooth.
4. Beat in your baking soda, baking powder and your salt until well combined.
5. Add the cocoa powder and then the oats in small batches, beating them until it is combined well and then beat in your almond milk.

6. Stir in your chocolate chips by and then roll your dough out by hand into small balls and place them on the baking sheet.
7. Flatten the cookies a little and then bake them for between 10 and 12 minutes until the edges are browned.

# Peanut Butter Chocolate Brownies

**Servings**: 10 to 12

**Ingredients**:

- 1 cup of canned coconut milk (light)
- ¼ cup of ground flaxseed
- 1 cup of vegan chocolate chips
- ½ cup of agave nectar
- 2 tablespoons of organic cane sugar

- 3 tablespoons of coconut oil
- 1 tablespoon of vanilla extract
- 1 cup minus 2 tablespoons of coconut flour
- 3 tablespoons of tapioca starch
- ½ teaspoon of baking powder
- ¼ teaspoon of baking soda
- ¼ teaspoon of salt
- 1/3 cup of all-natural peanut butter

**Instructions**:

1. Preheat your oven to a temperature of 375°F and place a piece of parchment paper on the bottom of a square baking pan – grease it with cooking spray.
2. Put your coconut milk in a saucepan and heat it until it steams.
3. Pour the milk into a bowl and stir in your flaxseed and vegan chocolate chips.
4. Let the chocolate chips melt and then stir in the agave, sugar and oil as well as the vanilla extract.
5. Let the mixture sit for 5 minutes while you stir together your coconut flour, tapioca starch, baking powder, baking soda, and salt.

6. Stir the dry ingredients into the chocolate mixture until it is combined well then pour the batter into your baking pan.
7. Melt your peanut butter in the microwave then drizzle it over the batter in your pan – use a knife to swirl it.
8. Bake the brownies for between 22 and 25 minutes and then let them cool completely before you slice them.

## *Gluten-Free Almond Cookies*

**Servings**: about 2 dozen

**Ingredients**:

- 3 cups of blanched almond flour
- ½ teaspoon of baking soda
- ½ teaspoon of ground cinnamon
- ½ teaspoon of salt
- ½ cup of agave nectar

- ¼ cup of melted coconut oil
- 1 cup of sliced almonds

**Instructions**:

1. Preheat your oven to a temperature of 325°F and place a piece of parchment paper on a cookie sheet.
2. Combine your almond flour and baking soda in a mixing bowl with your cinnamon and salt.
3. In another bowl, stir together your agave and coconut oil with your vanilla and almond extract.
4. Stir together your wet ingredient mix and the dry until it is combined well.
5. Spoon your batter onto the cookie sheet, using a heaping teaspoon.
6. Flatten each cookie a little bit by hand and then press a few slices of almond into the dough.
7. Bake your cookies for between 15 and 17 minutes until they are golden brown.

## *Maple Oatmeal Walnut Cookies*

**Servings**: 16 to 18

**Ingredients**:

- 1 tablespoon of ground flaxseed
- 3 tablespoons of warm water
- 2 cups of old-fashioned oats

- 1 cup of all-purpose gluten-free flour blend
- 1 ½ teaspoons of ground cinnamon
- ¾ teaspoon of baking soda
- Pinch of salt
- ½ cup of vegan butter at room temperature
- 1/3 cup of pure maple syrup
- 1 teaspoon of vanilla extract
- ½ cup of chopped up walnuts

**Instructions**:

1. Preheat your oven to a temperature of 350°F and place a piece of parchment paper on a baking sheet.
2. Stir together your flaxseed and your water in a small bowl and let it sit for 5 minutes.
3. In another bowl, stir your oats together with your gluten-free flour and your cinnamon, baking soda, and salt.
4. In a separate bowl, use a stand mixer or hand mixer to beat the vegan butter with the maple syrup until it is creamy.
5. Beat in your flaxseed mixture and the vanilla extract as well.
6. Slowly add your flour mixture while you are beating the batter until it is just combined.

7. Stir in your chopped up walnuts and then drop the cookie dough onto the cookie sheet.
8. Make each cookie about 2 tablespoons worth of dough.
9. Bake your cookies for between 15 and 20 minutes until the edges of them are golden brown.

# PART 3:

# Vegan Gluten-Free Cakes, Cupcakes and Quick Breads

## *Vegan Chocolate Cupcakes*

**Servings**: 12

**Ingredients**:

- 2 tablespoons ground flaxseed
- 5 tablespoons warm water
- ½ cup of unsweetened almond milk
- 1 teaspoon of apple cider vinegar
- 1 ½ teaspoons of baking soda

- 1/3 cup of organic cane sugar
- 5 tablespoons of agave nectar
- 1 cup of unsweetened applesauce
- ¼ cup of melted coconut oil
- Pinch of salt
- ½ cup of unsweetened cocoa powder
- ½ cup of blanched almond flour
- 4 tablespoons of oat flour
- ¾ cups of all-purpose gluten-free flour blend

**Instructions**:

1. Preheat your oven to a temperature of 375°F and line a 12-cup muffin pan using paper liners – you can also just spray it with cooking spray.
2. Whisk together your flaxseed and water in a large bowl and let it sit for 5 minutes.
3. Stir together your almond milk and vinegar in a small bowl and let it sit for 5 minutes then add the baking soda.
4. Add the almond milk mixture along with the sugar and agave to the flaxseed mixture and stir until combined well.
5. Stir in your applesauce along with your coconut oil and salt.

6. Add the cocoa powder and almond flour as well as your oat flour and gluten-free flour until it forms a nice batter.
7. Spoon the batter into the muffin pan, filling each cup about ¾ of the way full.
8. Bake your cupcakes for between 28 and 35 minutes or until a knife you insert into the middle comes out clean.

## *Gluten-Free Chocolate Zucchini Bread*

**Servings**: 8 to 10

**Ingredients**:

- 2 tablespoons of ground flaxseed
- 5 tablespoons of warm water
- 1 cup of organic cane sugar
- ¼ cup of melted coconut oil or olive oil
- ¼ cup of unsweetened applesauce
- 1 ½ cups of grated zucchini (squeezed to remove moisture)
- 1 ½ cups of all-purpose gluten-free flour blend
- ½ cup of blanched almond flour
- ½ cup of old-fashioned oats
- ¼ cup of cocoa powder (unsweetened)
- 1 ½ teaspoon of baking powder
- ¾ teaspoon of baking soda
- Pinch of salt

**Instructions**:

1. Preheat your oven to a temperature of 350°F and spray a regular loaf pan with cooking spray.
2. Whisk together your flaxseed and water in a small bowl then let it rest for 5 minutes.

3. In a large mixing bowl, combine your sugar and oil with your applesauce.
4. Stir in the flaxseed mixture and then fold in your shredded zucchini.
5. In another both, combine your gluten-free flour with your almond flour, oats and your cocoa powder and then stir in your baking soda, baking powder, and the salt.
6. Add the mixture of dry ingredients to the wet ingredients in small batches while stirring it very well.
7. Pour your finished batter into the loaf pan you prepared.
8. Bake your zucchini bread for 45 to 55 minutes or until a knife that you insert in the middle comes out clean.
9. Cool your bread in the pan for 5 to 10 minutes and then turn it out onto a cooling rack to finish cooling.

## Gluten-Free Sponge Cake

**Servings**: 8 to 10

**Ingredients**:

- 1 ½ cups of all-purpose gluten-free flour blend
- 1 cup of organic cane sugar
- 1 teaspoon of baking powder
- 1 teaspoon of baking soda
- 1 cup of unsweetened almond milk

- 6 tablespoons of melted coconut oil
- 1 tablespoon of vanilla extract
- 1 tablespoon of white vinegar

**Instructions**:

1. Preheat your oven to a temperature of 350°F and grease a round cake pan with cooking spray.
2. Combine your all-purpose gluten-free flour and your sugar in a mixing bowl along with your baking powder and baking soda.
3. In another bowl, whisk your almond milk and oil together with your vanilla extract and vinegar.
4. Stir your wet ingredients into your dry ingredient mixture until combined well – beat it for at least 3 minutes.
5. Pour your batter into the pan and bake it for between 45 and 60 minutes until it is fully cooked.
6. Let the cake cool in its pan for 10 minutes and then turn it out onto a cooling rack and cool the rest of the way.

## *Vanilla Bean Cupcakes*

**Servings**: 12

**Ingredients**:

- 1 cup of unsweetened almond milk
- 6 tablespoons of melted coconut oil
- 2 tablespoons of ground flaxseed
- 1 vanilla bean, split and seeds scraped
- 1 teaspoon of apple cider vinegar

- 2/3 cup of white rice flour
- 1/3 cup of blanched almond flour
- 1/3 cup of coconut flour
- 1/3 cup of tapioca starch
- ¾ cup of organic cane sugar
- ¼ teaspoon of xanthan gum
- 1 teaspoon of baking powder
- ¾ teaspoon of baking soda
- ½ teaspoon of salt

**Instructions**:

1. Preheat your oven to a temperature of 350°F and line a 12-cup muffin pan using paper liners – you can also just spray it with cooking spray.
2. Whisk together your almond milk and oil together with your flaxseed, vanilla bean, and cider vinegar.
3. In another bowl, stir together your rice flour, almond flour and coconut flour with the tapioca starch, sugar and xanthan gum.
4. Stir in your baking powder, baking soda and salt until combined well.
5. Add your wet ingredient mixture into your dry ingredient mixture and stir it up well.

6. Spoon the batter into the muffin pan, filling each cup about ¾ of the way full.
7. Bake your cupcakes for between 8 and 12 minutes or until a knife you insert into the middle comes out clean.
8. Garnish with a vegan gluten-free cream of your choice.

## *Easy Cinnamon Pumpkin Bread*

**Servings**: 8 to 10

**Ingredients**:

- 1 ½ tablespoons of ground flaxseed
- 2 ½ tablespoons of warm water
- 1 ½ cups of pumpkin puree
- ½ cup of light brown sugar, packed
- 3 tablespoons of agave nectar

- 3 tablespoons of melted coconut oil
- 1 tablespoon of baking powder
- 1 ½ teaspoons of ground cinnamon
- ½ teaspoon of ground nutmeg
- ½ teaspoon of salt
- ¾ cups of unsweetened almond milk
- 1 ½ cups of almond flour
- 1 cup of all-purpose gluten-free flour blend
- 1 ¼ cups of old-fashioned oats

**Instructions**:

1. Preheat your oven to a temperature of 350°F and cut a piece of parchment paper to size and place it on the bottom of a loaf pan – spray the rest with cooking spray.
2. Stir together your flaxseed and water in a small bowl and let it sit for 5 minutes.
3. Put your pumpkin puree in a bowl and stir in the sugar, agave, coconut oil, baking powder, cinnamon, nutmeg, and salt.
4. Stir in your flaxseed mixture as well as your almond milk until it is combined well.
5. In another bowl, stir your almond flour together with your all-purpose gluten-free flour and your oats.

6. Add the dry ingredients to your wet ingredient mixture and stir it into a batter.
7. Pour your batter into your loaf pan and spread it evenly.
8. Bake your pumpkin bread for between 1 hour and 1 hour 15 minutes until a knife that you insert in the middle comes out clean.
9. Cool your pumpkin bread for 10 minutes and then turn it out onto a cooling rack and cool it the rest of the way.

## *Chocolate Coconut Cupcakes*

**Servings**: 12

**Ingredients**:

- 2 tablespoons ground flaxseed
- 5 tablespoons warm water
- ½ cup of unsweetened almond milk
- 1 teaspoon of apple cider vinegar
- 1 ½ teaspoons of baking soda
- 1 teaspoon coconut extract

- 1/3 cup of organic cane sugar
- 5 tablespoons of agave nectar
- 1 cup of unsweetened applesauce
- ¼ cup of melted coconut oil
- Pinch of salt
- ½ cup of unsweetened cocoa powder
- ½ cup of blanched almond flour
- 4 tablespoons of oat flour
- ¾ cups of all-purpose gluten-free flour blend
- ½ cup of unsweetened shredded coconut

**Instructions**:

1. Preheat your oven to a temperature of 375°F and line a 12-cup muffin pan using paper liners – you can also just spray it with cooking spray.
2. Whisk together your flaxseed and water in a large bowl and let it sit for 5 minutes.
3. Stir together your almond milk and vinegar in a small bowl and let it sit for 5 minutes then add the baking soda and coconut extract.
4. Add the almond milk mixture along with the sugar and agave to the flaxseed mixture and stir until combined well.

5. Stir in your applesauce along with your coconut oil and salt.
6. Add the cocoa powder and almond flour as well as your oat flour, gluten-free flour and shredded coconut until it forms a nice batter.
7. Spoon the batter into the muffin pan, filling each cup about ¾ of the way full.
8. Bake your cupcakes for between 28 and 35 minutes or until a knife you insert into the middle comes out clean.

## *Vanilla Strawberry Sheet Cake*

**Servings**: 10 to 12

**Ingredients**:

- 1 cup of unsweetened almond milk
- 6 tablespoons of melted coconut oil
- 2 tablespoons of ground flaxseed
- 1 vanilla bean, split and seeds scraped
- 1 teaspoon of apple cider vinegar

- 2/3 cup of white rice flour
- 1/3 cup of blanched almond flour
- 1/3 cup of coconut flour
- 1/3 cup of tapioca starch
- ¾ cup of organic cane sugar
- ¼ teaspoon of xanthan gum
- 1 teaspoon of baking powder
- ¾ teaspoon of baking soda
- ½ teaspoon of salt
- 1 cup of sliced strawberries

**Instructions**:

1. Preheat your oven to a temperature of 350°F and line the bottom of a 9x11-inch baking pan with parchment.
2. Whisk together your almond milk and oil together with your flaxseed, vanilla bean, and cider vinegar.
3. In another bowl, stir together your rice flour, almond flour and coconut flour with the tapioca starch, sugar and xanthan gum.
4. Stir in your baking powder, baking soda and salt until combined well.
5. Add your wet ingredient mixture into your dry ingredient mixture and stir it up well.

6. Spoon the batter into the baking pan and spread it evenly. Sprinkle the sliced strawberries over top.
7. Bake your cake for between 20 and 30 minutes or until a knife you insert into the middle comes out clean.

# Gluten-Free Carob Chip Banana Bread

**Servings**: 8 to 10

**Ingredients**:

- 1 ½ tablespoons of ground flaxseed
- 2 ½ tablespoons of warm water
- 1 ½ cups of mashed-up bananas
- ½ cup of organic cane sugar
- 3 tablespoons of agave nectar

- 3 tablespoons of melted coconut oil
- 1 tablespoon of baking powder
- 1 teaspoon of ground cinnamon
- ½ teaspoon of salt
- ¾ cups of unsweetened almond milk
- 1 ½ cups of almond flour
- 1 cup of all-purpose gluten-free flour blend
- 1 ¼ cups of old-fashioned oats
- ½ cup of carob chips (mini, if you can find them)

**Instructions**:

1. Preheat your oven to a temperature of 350°F and cut a piece of parchment paper to size and place it on the bottom of a loaf pan – spray the rest with cooking spray.
2. Stir together your flaxseed and water in a small bowl and let it sit for 5 minutes.
3. Put your mashed-up banana in a bowl and stir in the sugar, agave, coconut oil, baking powder, cinnamon, and salt.
4. Stir in your flaxseed mixture as well as your almond milk until it is combined well.
5. In another bowl, stir your almond flour together with your all-purpose gluten-free flour and your oats.

6. Add the dry ingredients to your wet ingredient mixture and stir it into a batter.
7. Pour your batter into your loaf pan and spread it evenly then sprinkle the carob chips on stop.
8. Bake your banana bread for between 1 hour and 1 hour 15 minutes until a knife that you insert in the middle comes out clean.
9. Cool your banana bread for 10 minutes and then turn it out onto a cooling rack and cool it the rest of the way.

## *Raspberry Coconut Cupcakes*

**Servings**: 12

**Ingredients**:

- 1 cup of unsweetened almond milk
- 6 tablespoons of melted coconut oil
- 2 tablespoons of ground flaxseed
- 1 teaspoon vanilla extract
- 1 teaspoon of apple cider vinegar

- 1 cup of white rice flour
- 1/3 cup of coconut flour
- 1/3 cup of arrowroot powder
- ¾ cup of organic cane sugar
- ¼ teaspoon of xanthan gum
- 1 teaspoon of baking powder
- ¾ teaspoon of baking soda
- ½ teaspoon of salt
- 1 cup of fresh raspberries
- ½ cup of unsweetened shredded coconut

**Instructions**:

1. Preheat your oven to a temperature of 350°F and line a 12-cup muffin pan using paper liners – you can also just spray it with cooking spray.
2. Whisk together your almond milk and oil together with your flaxseed, vanilla extract, and cider vinegar.
3. In another bowl, stir together your rice flour, and coconut flour with the arrowroot powder, sugar and xanthan gum.
4. Stir in your baking powder, baking soda and salt until combined well.
5. Add your wet ingredient mixture into your dry ingredient mixture and stir it up well.

6. Stir in your raspberries and the shredded coconut.
7. Spoon the batter into the muffin pan, filling each cup about ¾ of the way full.
8. Bake your cupcakes for between 8 and 12 minutes or until a knife you insert into the middle comes out clean.

# *Lemon Blueberry Cake*

**Servings**: 10 to 12

**Ingredients**:

- 1 cup of unsweetened almond milk
- 2 teaspoons of white vinegar
- 1 ½ cups of tapioca flour
- 1 ½ cups of white rice flour
- 1 cup of sorghum flour

- 2 cups of organic cane sugar
- 2 ½ teaspoons of baking soda
- 1 ½ teaspoons of baking powder
- 2 teaspoons of xanthan gum
- 1 teaspoon of salt
- 2 cups of warm water
- ½ cup of unsweetened applesauce
- 1/3 cup of melted coconut oil
- ¼ cup of fresh lemon juice
- 2 tablespoons of fresh lemon zest
- 1 ½ cups of fresh blueberries

**Instructions:**

1. Preheat your oven to a temperature of 350°F and grease a 9x13-inch rectangular baking pan with cooking spray.
2. Stir together your almond milk and your vinegar in a small bowl and set it aside.
3. Combine your flours and sugar in a large mixing bowl along with your baking powder, baking soda, xanthan gum, and salt.
4. Stir in your almond milk mixture along with your water, applesauce, and coconut oil.

5. Add the lemon juice and lemon zest and stir until it is combined well.
6. Fold in your fresh blueberries and then spread the batter in the cake pan.
7. Bake your cake for between 25 and 35 minutes until a knife inserted in the middle comes out clean and the edges are browned.

# Vegan Cinnamon Zucchini Bread

**Servings**: 8 to 10

**Ingredients**:

- 2 tablespoons of ground flaxseed
- 5 tablespoons of warm water
- 1 cup of organic cane sugar
- ¼ cup of melted coconut oil or olive oil
- ¼ cup of unsweetened applesauce

- 1 ½ cups of grated zucchini (squeezed to remove moisture)
- 1 ½ cups of all-purpose gluten-free flour blend
- ½ cup of blanched almond flour
- ½ cup of old-fashioned oats
- 1 ½ teaspoon of baking powder
- ¾ teaspoon of baking soda
- 1 ½ teaspoons of ground cinnamon

**Instructions**:

1. Preheat your oven to a temperature of 350°F and spray a regular loaf pan with cooking spray.
2. Whisk together your flaxseed and water in a small bowl then let it rest for 5 minutes.
3. In a large mixing bowl, combine your sugar and oil with your applesauce.
4. Stir in the flaxseed mixture and then fold in your shredded zucchini.
5. In another both, combine your gluten-free flour with your almond flour and oats then stir in your baking soda, baking powder, and the cinnamon.
6. Add the mixture of dry ingredients to the wet ingredients in small batches while stirring it very well.
7. Pour your finished batter into the loaf pan you prepared.

8. Bake your zucchini bread for 45 to 55 minutes or until a knife that you insert in the middle comes out clean.
9. Cool your bread in the pan for 5 to 10 minutes and then turn it out onto a cooling rack to finish cooling.

Before you go, I'd like to remind you that there is a free, complimentary eBook waiting for you. Download it today to treat yourself to healthy, gluten-free desserts and snacks so that you never feel deprived again!

**Download link**

http://bit.ly/gluten-free-desserts-book

# Conclusion

So, how was your baking party?

Did you enjoy my recipes?

Which one was your favorite?

Preparation is the key to success. If you are on a busy schedule (like me and my family) make sure you do your vegan/gluten-free baking on the weekends. It's a great way to socialize with your family and friends. You can also get them involved.

Final words: While the gluten-free diet is a medical treatment for individuals with celiac disease or gluten intolerance, it can be beneficial for nearly everyone. Before you decide whether the gluten-free diet is the right choice for you, take the time to learn as much as you can about the diet including its benefits, its risks, and which foods you can and cannot eat.

One more thing- there are different kinds of gluten-free diets (for example Paleo, vegetarian, vegan). You don't have to go 100% vegan to enjoy a gluten-free diet as it can be personalized. It's totally up to you. However, I believe that we should all learn more vegan options and reduce the consumption of animal products.

This does not have to be painful as there are many delicious, plant-based options out there.

My main focus, as an author, is to create helpful and information gluten-free and anti-inflammatory recipe books that can accommodate vegans, vegetarians and paleo diet enthusiasts. I am always open to new suggestions so if you are looking for anything specific, please send me an e-mail and let me know:

**kira.novac@kiraglutenfreerecipes.com**

I am here to help you.

This is how I wrote this book. After I released the book: "Gluten-Free Baking Cookbook: Delicious and Healthy, 100% Gluten-Free Cake & Bake Recipes You Will Love" that contains more traditional, family gluten-free recipes (not for vegans), many readers asked me for more vegan options (vegan and gluten-free at the same time). This is exactly what I did and I hope that you will enjoy them as well. With vegan, gluten-free dessert options you don't need to feel deprived as you can enjoy variety and taste while taking care of your health as well…

Me and my family follow gluten-free diets (a few years ago my son was diagnosed with celiac, also called celiac sprue, disease and, so we had to go gluten-free), and we also have close family members and friends who are vegan. This is why I had to learn how to combine both diets so that we can enjoy healthy and delicious meals together. Thanks to my vegan friends, I also realized that I need to reduce the consumption of animal products and discover more vegan options (even though I am not 100% vegan).

If you decide that the gluten-free diet is the diet for you and you also want to keep it vegan, I hope you will try some of the recipes in this book as you transition into the diet. Please let me know your favorites- **the review section of this book** is an excellent place to share your experience with other readers.

# To post an honest review

One more thing… If you have received any value from this book, can you please rank it and post a short review? It only takes a few seconds really and it would really make my day. It's you I am writing for and your opinion is always much appreciated. In order to do so;

1. Log into your account
2. Search for my book on Amazon or check your orders/ or go to my author page at:

   http://amazon.com/author/kira-novac

3. Click on a book you have read, then click on "reviews" and "create your review".

# Recommended Reading

Book Link:

http://bit.ly/gluten-free-vegan

# Recommended Reading

Book Link:

http://bit.ly/vegan-spiralizer

# FOR MORE HEALTH BOOKS (KINDLE & PAPERBACK) BY KIRA NOVAC PLEASE VISIT:

## *www.kiraglutenfreerecipes.com/books*

Thank you for taking an interest in my work,

Kira and Holistic Wellness Books

**HOLISTIC WELLNESS & HEALTH BOOKS**

*If you are interested in health, wellness, spirituality and personal development, visit our page and be the first one to know about free and 0.99 eBooks:*

www.HolisticWellnessBooks.com

www.ingramcontent.com/pod-product-compliance
Lightning Source LLC
Chambersburg PA
CBHW072205100526
44589CB00015B/2378